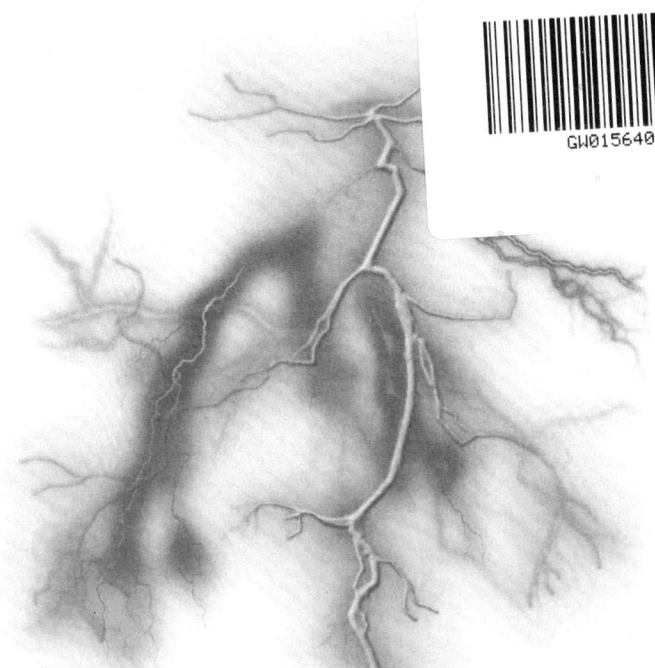

OUT OF THE STORM
Becoming strong disciples

Richard George

short course

The way of
THE SPIRIT

resources@thewayofthespirit.com
www.thewayofthespirit.com

1st Edition Published in Great Britain in 2016
by The Way of the Spirit, Norfolk, UK

Copyright © 2016 Richard George

All rights reserved. No part of this publication may be reproduced, stored in a retrieval system, or transmitted, in any form or by any means, electronic, mechanical, photocopying, recording or otherwise, without the permission, in writing, of the publisher.

ISBN 978-1-9085-2817-9

Scripture taken from the
HOLY BIBLE, NEW INTERNATIONAL VERSION.
Copyright © 1973, 1978, 1984 by International Bible Society. Used by permission of Hodder and Stoughton Limited.

Bible Reading Course

The purpose of this booklet and the recorded teaching that goes with it is partly to give you some impression of how The Way of the Spirit Bible Reading Course works. It is not, however, just an excerpt or collection of excerpts from the fuller course, but a properly integrated short course in its own right, and as such is somewhat different in presentation.

- The full course takes you systematically through the whole Bible, chapter by chapter, with the help of a textbook; here you have only a little booklet giving a brief survey of a Bible theme.
- The full course has more comprehensive worksheets.
- The course recordings offer more systematic teaching arranged in twenty-minute parts.

Nevertheless, by using these materials you should capture the flavour of the full course quite well. The purpose of The Way of the Spirit is to help Christians tap into the life that is to be found in the Bible and the power of the Spirit revealed in its pages, to help you understand what the Bible is all about, what the way of God's Spirit is in it, and how to enter more fully into the richness of life men of Bible-times enjoyed. You should find all these aims met in some measure as you use **OUT OF THE STORM**.

If after completing this short study you wish to proceed to the fuller course, please e-mail us at resources@thewayofthespirit.com or visit our web site at www.thewayofthespirit.com

May God bless you richly as you study his Word.

How to Use This Booklet

This booklet is arranged in two parts:

- The first (pages 1-33) introduces the study.
- The second (pages 34-51) is a six-part question sheet.

Recorded teaching to accompany the booklet is also available.[1]

You can use this booklet in several different ways:

- By itself with your Bible.
- Along with the recorded teaching and your Bible.
- By studying in a group.

Whichever method you choose, learn to listen for what the Holy Spirit has to tell you—about your beliefs, attitudes and life-style. Ask yourself what lessons you should be learning from your readings, so that you can apply them to your own understanding and life as a Christian.

Part Two, the study guide, has introductory notes on page 34 with further suggestions about how to use it. Each part of this section has questions that will help

---

[1] You can listen to or download the teaching free of charge from our website at www.thewayofthespirit.com/audio. You can also buy the teaching on audio CDs by emailing resources@thewayofthespirit.com.

you determine what you have learned and encourage you to apply that in practical living.

The notes have been prepared in such a way that you can use them privately or in a group. Experience has shown that group study is much more fruitful.

If you use the recorded teaching, you may find it helpful to listen to the relevant part before starting your readings, but if so you should also listen to it again afterwards.

If you use this booklet in a group, you will need to listen to the recording early in your meeting. Then discuss your answers to the questions, share your insights and encourage one another to grow in the Lord. Remember to allow time for prayer and fellowship as well.

1.

OUT OF THE STORM PART ONE

INTRODUCTION

Well-fed sheep survive storms.

His way is in the whirlwind and the storm.[2]

Disciples of Jesus often do not have easy lives; there are storms to navigate.

When storms punctuate our Christian journeys we need a right approach towards them. We would like to avoid them altogether and although many are avoidable, others are clearly not, they seem to come out of nowhere and hit us. We can learn to avoid some storms, but need to accept that others are an integral and inevitable part of being a disciple.

In Matthew's gospel we read how Jesus teaches about the cost of following him: He tells a budding disciple

---

[2] Nahum 1.3c.

OUT OF THE STORM
Becoming strong disciples

he must be prepared to have nowhere to sleep, and seems to rebuke another for prioritising the funeral of his recently deceased father, though possibly the disciple is asking to wait until the day his father is no longer alive.[3] In either case Jesus' reply *Follow me, and let the dead bury their own dead*[4] seems tough, highlighting the reality of what following him might mean. Then in the verses immediately after (in some translations these verses are misleadingly separated from those preceding by a heading), Matthew describes the disciples following Jesus onto a boat.[5] What happens next is unexpected: without warning a furious storm comes upon the lake. This is what happens when you follow Jesus, Matthew seems to be saying, he'll lead you into storms.

The frightened disciples waken Jesus and ask for his help, and he rebukes them for their lack of faith. In due course they will become individuals filled with the Holy Spirit who fearlessly advance Jesus' message of the Kingdom into and through every storm, but more of that later.

There is another storm mentioned in Matthew prior to this episode in the boat.[6] In a parable told by Jesus two men built a house, each upon different foundations. Some Bible stories are so familiar to us that we miss their point. We may vaguely think that in

---

[3] Matthew 8.18-22
[4] Matthew 8.22
[5] Matthew 8.23-27
[6] Matthew 7.24-29

OUT OF THE STORM
Becoming strong disciples

this parable Jesus was teaching that 'Christians' will stand the storms of life better than those who are not. But in the parable both builders are Christian. Both could be keen, regular church-goers and active in church life. Both could be filled with the Holy Spirit, hear God's words, and engage regularly in Bible studies. What matters though, Jesus is saying, is not whether we hear God's words, but what we do once we've heard them: *Therefore everyone who hears these words of mine* **and puts them into practice** *is like a wise man who built his house on the rock. The rain came down, the streams rose, and the winds blew and beat against that house; yet it did not fall, because it had its foundation on the rock. But everyone who hears these words of mine* **and does not put them into practice** *is like a foolish man who built his house on sand. The rain came down, the streams rose, and the winds blew and beat against that house, and it fell with a great crash.*[7]

Those who live their lives listening for, hearing and *then doing* what God says, are the ones who build on the rock. The rock here is not Christ, but doing what Christ says. To be upon the rock is to hear his words and put them into practice; to obey God's words is the key, not merely to hear them. We're called, not merely to listen and give mental assent, but to live our lives by them; to choose to believe them, letting them determine the direction of the steps we take. The

---

[7] Matt 7.24-27

OUT OF THE STORM
Becoming strong disciples

parable of the two builders, followed soon after by the disciples following Jesus into the storm, implies that storms are unavoidable. They are going to happen. It is how we have lived our lives prior to the storm arriving, and what we do now it's arrived, that will determine what impact the storm is allowed to make upon us. Will our house stand or fall?

There is a crucial pastoral note to make here: well-fed sheep survive storms. So many of our storms would have been less damaging had our foundations been properly in place. Part of the teacher/pastor's responsibility is to equip people to build strong foundations in their lives before the crisis hits, training them to hear the truth of Jesus' words and obey them. When the storms arrive they are not as devastating when we're firmly and confidently living on that rock.

In the pages which follow we will look at some storms in the Bible: one that was certainly avoidable, some that come directly as a result of following Jesus, and others sent by our adversary, who wishes above all else to stop us bearing fruit in our lives. We will also consider some practical steps we can take when we're in the middle of a storm, no matter what its origin or cause.

Chapter One

Avoidable storms – Jonah

> To be called and used by God in any way is always an awesome matter, and often costly.

The word of the Lord came to... is the standard way of introducing a prophet in the Old Testament. The book of Jonah opens with God's word coming to him in the form of a command. Jonah is a prophet and God commands him to prophesy: to go to the foreign city of Nineveh, the capital of Assyria, and preach repentance.

To understand what this command may have meant to Jonah, we can read Nahum describing Nineveh in Jonah's time: *Woe to the city of blood, full of lies, full of plunder, never without victims!... Many casualties, piles of dead bodies without number– people stumbling over the corpses ... "I am against you" declares the Lord Almighty.*[8]

No wonder Jonah is reluctant to go there; it was a brutal place and the Assyrians could be a brutal people. In Jonah's time, Assyria was the world superpower, in stark contrast to a tiny and relatively insignificant Israel. Further, it was rare to see

---

[8] Nahum 3.1-5

OUT OF THE STORM
Becoming strong disciples

Israelites being sent to other peoples, so Jonah had few precedents to encourage him.[9]

The prophet Jonah doubts that God's idea is a good one, and he runs away. He heads for the port where he can catch a boat to Tarshish, present-day Spain. He goes *down* to Joppa, a port, *down* to a boat, *down* below deck and soon *down* into a deep sleep. Eventually he will go even further downwards, into the sea. It's clear what happens to those who run away from the Lord's commands: they go down. Jonah has run away from God's commands and his storm approaches.

The narrative swiftly moves along. God sends a great wind which causes a violent storm. The sailors are afraid; Jonah is asleep. This may remind us of another who slept on a boat during a storm, but Jesus' sleep is entirely different, he remained at peace and slept on the boat during the storm because of his faith, Jonah's sleep was due to fear, escapism and denial.

Jonah wasn't allowed to slumber through the storm, because the sailors, who feared the storm, woke him – as the disciples would one day wake Jesus. They asked who his god was, for theirs could not quell the storm. In an age when nations had many gods, Israel stood out by worshipping only one. The sailors didn't know where Jonah came from or, apparently,

---

[9] This partly explains why we don't see Jews going out to make converts today: it has not been part of their tradition or worldview to do so.

OUT OF THE STORM
Becoming strong disciples

anything about his God. *I am a Hebrew and I worship the Lord, the God of heaven, who made the sea and the land.*[10] They were terrified by this, for they had never heard or even conceived of a deity who had created the world.

Jonah asked to be thrown overboard, but the sailors, reluctant to do this, attempted to row back to safety. (I'm reminded of an animated version of Jonah I used to watch with my then young children. The sailors dipped Jonah in and out of the sea, and when any part of his body touched water the storm immediately ceased and there was blue sky and sunshine. The moment they lifted him out of the water, the dark clouds blew in and the torrential wind and rain returned. The weather alternated between storm and sunshine as they kept dipping him in and out).

Eventually as the sea grew even wilder, the sailors had no choice but to follow Jonah's suggestion. As soon as they threw him in the storm calmed. As Jonah later recounted, he sank down, into the depths of the ocean. As he fell through the water, and as the seaweed wrapped itself around his neck he finally turned back to God in repentance and faith. God heard his cry, sent the whale (or at least a big fish), and Jonah was rescued. As in the story which we call the parable of the prodigal son, it was only when the one running away turned, acknowledged his sin and repented, that he discovered his loving father waiting,

---

[10] Jonah 1.9

OUT OF THE STORM
Becoming strong disciples

with welcoming arms outstretched. In the New Testament parable, the father doesn't wait for him to arrive home, he even ran towards him.

Sin and repentance can sometimes be left out from popular religion and contemporary expressions of Christianity. Yet without it there can be no individual or corporate revival. The moment we move towards God and truly repent, we discover he is already running in our direction. God is totally unmoved by fashionable spiritual trends and popular opinion that seek, sometimes, to replace true repentance.

Three days later the whale delivered Jonah to land, vomited him onto the beach, and God commanded him, as before, to go to Assyria. This time, in great fear of the Lord, he obeyed and went to Nineveh (he had gained nothing by running away, Nineveh was a long way from the beach). Arriving there he preached the rather minimalistic word God had given him: *Forty more days and Nineveh will be overturned.*[11] As he spoke, revival came to the city; even the king repented and covered himself with sackcloth and ashes.

Who could have blamed him from running away from such a task? But, as Paul would later write, *God's gifts and his call are irrevocable,*[12] so he could never escape by running away from them. Jonah's storm was

---

[11] Jonah 3.4
[12] Romans 11.29

OUT OF THE STORM
Becoming strong disciples

brought entirely upon himself by his reluctance to follow God's command. But, as he eventually discovered, when God calls he equips, provides and protects. As a prophet Jonah should have known this, and that therefore he could never escape by running away from them. In any case, as the psalmist expressed, *where can I flee from your presence?*[13]

The anointing to speak God's words is not given for our own pleasure or satisfaction but to enable God's work, the extension of his Kingdom. To be called and used by him in any way is always an awesome matter, and often costly.

In these days, intimacy and fellowship with God is enjoyed and celebrated in a close and personal relationship with Jesus. But as we consider his bigness, otherness and holiness, we would do well to remember the other side of the coin too. As one New Testament writer puts it: *it is a dreadful thing to fall into the hands of the living God.*[14]

---

[13] Psalm 139.7
[14] Hebrews 10.31

OUT OF THE STORM
Becoming strong disciples

Chapter Two

Caught in a storm – Paul

This journey in chains, far from being a defeat or set-back to Paul's ministry, served to extend the reach of the gospel.

Paul was a man who followed Jesus; he followed him steadfastly as Israel had once followed the cloud of glory. He was not put off by painful experiences, by persecution, or warnings from the Holy Spirit about danger ahead; indeed, he seemed to have few concerns for his own well-being. The last section of the book of Acts describes Paul in custody and experiencing events that are somewhat reminiscent of the legal trials Jesus had had to endure. A variety of men – Felix, Festus and Agrippa – heard Paul in Caesarea before finally sending him to Rome to be tried by Caesar, which was his right as a Roman citizen.

Paul set sail to Rome under the custody of Centurion Julius, who showed Paul kindness and respect. After one or two changes of ship they hit bad weather. Paul was quick to discern the danger ahead, though neither Julius nor the ship's captain listened to him. Paul warned them that their lives and cargo were at risk if they continued, but they did not see the danger themselves. Paul spoke clearly but no-one listened, and as they so often do, the loudest voices won the day.

OUT OF THE STORM
Becoming strong disciples

The storm grew and the ship took a violent battering. Just as those on Jonah's ship once did, the crew began throwing the cargo overboard. *When neither sun nor stars appeared for many days and the storm continued raging, [they] finally gave up all hope of being saved.*[15] But Paul, far from sleeping below deck, had seen it all coming, and with some authority stood and addressed the crew: *Men you should have taken my advice not to sail from Crete; then you would have spared yourselves this damage and loss. But now I urge you to keep up your courage, because not one of you will be lost; only the ship will be destroyed. Last night an angel of the God whose I am and whom I serve stood beside me and said 'Do not be afraid Paul. You must stand trial before Caesar; and God has graciously given you the lives of all who sail with you.' So keep up your courage, men, for I have faith in God that it will happen just as he told me. Nevertheless, we must run aground on some island.*[16]

The men had little time to think about his message as the storm blew on, unabated, for fourteen days. During this time, they ate nothing and barely slept. Paul endured the two-week day and night storm alongside everyone else, maintained by the strengthening and encouragement that came from the prophetic word he had received from the angel. At one point some of the crew attempted to leave the ship by lifeboat. Paul advised the soldiers not to let

---

[15] Acts 27.20
[16] Acts 27.21-26

OUT OF THE STORM
Becoming strong disciples

them go for they needed all hands on deck, and now they listened to him. They cut the ropes tying the lifeboats to the ship to prevent their escape.

Paul appears to have no thought for his forthcoming fate in Rome. Now, instead of worrying he broke bread with the sailors, just as Jesus once did before meeting his fate on the cross. The next day the ship broke up as it ran aground on Malta but no lives were lost, just as Paul had prophesied. The soldiers wanted to kill the prisoners, including Paul, to prevent them from escaping, but the centurion stopped them. Once on shore, Paul, instead of trying to escape, healed many of the sick on the island and even survived a snake attack. The life of the Kingdom thus continued to be expressed through Paul on Malta, as on the ship. Three months later another boat picked them up and delivered them to Rome.

Paul and those with him survived the storm. A deadly snake did not kill him, God was with him, sending him an angel when he needed one, and otherwise protecting him from all serious harm until his mission was completed. Even though a prisoner, he bore fruit on the journey, and walked with authority and stature. He had the courage and boldness to speak out prophetically, and as a true prophet, his prophecies came to pass. Many who met him came to enjoy the life of the Spirit flowing from him.

This journey in chains, far from being a defeat or setback to Paul's ministry, served to extend the reach of the gospel. It created an opportunity to preach and

OUT OF THE STORM
Becoming strong disciples

minister in the world's greatest city, Rome, providing the climax to Luke's epic two-part saga, Luke-Acts. Even under house arrest, he preached freely for two years. Despite losing his freedom, Paul now delivered the good news of Jesus and the Kingdom of God on Caesar's doorstep. It was a great victory: the gospel had reached Rome.

The storm that destroyed Paul's boat en route to Rome was no Jonah storm. Paul wasn't running away, so he didn't end up in it through his own disobedience. In fact, just as with the disciples on the lake of Galilee, it came as a result of following Jesus. And, by his courage and faith, he emerged victorious from it.

Chapter Three

A Perfect Storm – Jesus

> *[Jesus] kept his heart right and remained on course throughout to reach his goal, the cross, walking in perfect obedience.*

When Jesus entered Jerusalem on a donkey, the city was a cauldron of conflicting political, religious and divine aspiration. Quite knowingly, he was riding into a storm –a metaphorical storm – but no less fierce and threatening than any we've considered so far. The relentless winds of Rome's military and political machine, beating against Israel's heated expectation of liberation from slavery and oppression, would now create a perfect storm. God's plan to use one man to bring Israel's history to a climax was to be realised.

OUT OF THE STORM
Becoming strong disciples

Jesus knew exactly what he was riding into. Against all human logic as well as the advice, and pleadings of his closest disciples, he had chosen to leave Galilee and travel to Jerusalem, and had set his face like flint as he travelled there. He did not let anything, not even his family and friends, divert him.

His life and ministry came from his relationship with God. He often rose early in the morning and went to pray, he listened to his father's will above that of others; he was a man of prayer and obedience. His priority was to complete God's plan for his life. John's gospel especially makes it abundantly clear that Jesus' ministry flowed from his relationship with God. It was his obedience that made him a friend of God.

Up to this point God had protected him in every storm. He had saved him from attempts upon his life by Herod, crowds who tried to throw him off a cliff, and soldiers sent to arrest him. Then, his time had not yet come, but now it had, and God would allow him to be tried, tortured and sent to the cross.

As he lived out these last days we are struck by his stalwartness, his unruffled responses to the various characters who played a part in it all, and the single-mindedness with which he would now move towards his destiny. In John's gospel, at least, he is never portrayed as a victim but always as one who remains in charge, even while being tried and murdered on the cross. <u>Without a hint of self-interest</u>, only one thing matters, and that's fulfilling his destiny, to bring to fulfilment the ministry his father has given him. He

OUT OF THE STORM
Becoming strong disciples

walked through these stormy days serenely, despite the agony they brought. He kept his eyes on his father, never faltering. He healed the people and preached the Kingdom to the very end.

We have considered some of these scenes in earlier The Way of the Spirit short courses[17]: his trial before Herod and Pilate and, of course, the cross itself. Once we comprehend the reality of Jesus' true humanity[18] (not the half-man, half-God sort of figure many imagine), we realise how remarkable this walk was, and how real the storm was that he went through. Consider, for instance, the garden scene at Gethsemane, in which Jesus struggled with his approaching martyrdom as any man would. Yet he kept his heart right and remained on course throughout to reach his goal, the cross, walking in perfect obedience. He went there for the joy set before him, even when his closest friends deserted him, weathering the storm.

Jesus' storm arose because he walked obediently in God's will. This storm, however, didn't appear to have a happy ending, or produce the same fruit that Paul's storm produced. If we judged the outcome of Jesus' ministry by the scene around the cross, we would think he had failed completely. But Jesus had never focused on what others thought of him or his

---

[17] See *Behold the Man, Following the Lamb* and *Five Smooth Stones*.
[18] See *Behold the Man*, Richard George, published by The Way of the Spirit 2002.

ministry, he always chose to keep his eyes on the way ahead, trusting God to bring forth the fruit of his choosing.

Chapter Four

Out of the storm – Job

> *The first step to take in any storm ... is always the same: to look to God, to fix our eyes on him and meet with him afresh.*

In the first chapter of Job we see that it is Satan who is responsible for the storm which will engulf Job. This first scene is played out in heaven, like an operatic overture that the audience alone hears but is unheard by the actors, yet to come on stage. Satan presented himself before God and, when God described Job as a *blameless and upright man who fear(ed) God and shun(ned) evil,*[19] Satan challenged him. He suggested that Job's faithfulness depended only upon the blessings he had received from God. But would Job still live righteously if all was not going well? So God gave Satan permission to take away the blessings he had received to see what Job was really made of.

Enter the demonic storm: Job's property and livestock were attacked by invaders and destroyed, and when a mighty wind swept in from the desert all his children died. But he continued to speak well of the Lord, despite the trauma and devastation. Satan came before God again, now arguing that Job would surely

---

[19] Job 1.1

OUT OF THE STORM
Becoming strong disciples

crack if he experienced personal suffering. This time God granted him permission to strike Job himself, provided only that his life was spared. Satan afflicted him with disease, producing painful sores over his whole body.

Job fell from being one of the most blessed men in the land to being a childless invalid without wealth or property. He was now in great physical pain too, left to scrape his sores as he sat in an ash heap. His wife urged him to curse God and die, but he refused to do that despite not knowing the true cause of the storm.

Much of the rest of the book is taken up with Job's three friends expressing their opinions about why these bad things had happened to an apparently righteous man. In the nine speeches that follow, the clear message is that it must have been Job's fault. He must somehow have offended God.

But their words of wisdom failed to satisfy Job. His questions remained unanswered and he grew increasingly frustrated. Meanwhile, a younger man, Elihu (mentioned for the first time in chapter 32), waited his turn to speak. When he finally did get his chance, his words struck a different tone, for *it is the Spirit in a man, the breath of the Almighty that gives him understanding ... inside I am like bottled-up wine, like new wineskins ready to burst. I must speak and find relief; I must open my lips and reply.*[20] As Elihu

---

[20] Job 32.8,18-20

OUT OF THE STORM
Becoming strong disciples

(John McKay's so called proto-charismatic), continues his speech, his words are directed towards God and his creation. This is in stark contrast to the friends' counsel, who prefer to analyse Job's character.

As Elihu lifts their eyes to God, a storm is brewing. *Who can understand how he spreads out the clouds, how he thunders form the pavilion? See how he scatters his lightning about him, bathing the depths of the sea.*[21]

At this my heart pounds, and leaps from its place. Listen! Listen to the roar of his voice, to the rumbling that comes from his mouth. He unleashes his lighting beneath the whole heaven and sends it to the ends of the earth[22].

They are now focusing upon God himself rather than on Job's quandary; *Then the Lord answered Job out of the storm.*[23] God himself now speaks to them – for the first time in the book. Silent through Job's and his friend's arguments, God now responds to Elihu.

As we point out to the budding preachers and teachers in our full time school here in Norfolk, this is a stunning example of prophetic Bible teaching: Elihu starts his speech, or sermon perhaps, by lifting Job's eyes to God, despite and regardless of the personal storm Job is experiencing. It is now God's voice that is heard as he seamlessly continues Elihu's sermon. He

---

[21] Job 36.29-30
[22] Job 37.1-3
[23] Job 38.1

OUT OF THE STORM
Becoming strong disciples

describes awesome creatures and other things in his creation, and as they gaze upon them, and hear God's rhetorical questions (*where were you when I laid the earth's foundations?*[24]), his power, mystery and authority are glimpsed. As Job listens to God's words, he is forever transformed by this encounter with God. *My ears had heard of you but now my eyes have seen you.*[25] He had been a good man and thought he had known about godly things, but now he had encountered God and had no more to say.

He never did learn what caused the devastation in his life, and it no longer mattered, for the encounter had brought knowledge of a different kind, which needed no further explanation and demolished every self-justifying argument or pretension.

Elihu shows us the first step in escaping storms sent by Satan, which is to look up, to and at God, who is always bigger than, and above, any such storm. He is, after all, creator of all things – including the creature Satan. We need to let the Holy Spirit lead us into lifting our God-thoughts above the mundane and ordinary. We must allow him to remind us continually that God is beyond our rational and limited thinking. God is always ready to break in and show us new and even more wonderful things about himself, no matter

---

[24] Job 38.4
[25] Job 42.5

OUT OF THE STORM
Becoming strong disciples

how much or little, earthly or religious, wisdom we have accumulated.

In our relativistic western culture, it is fashionable to limit our experience and knowledge of God to subjective ways. But God is objective not subjective, and in this passage God breaks into Job's world from outside. The encounter originated in God, not Job's thinking or deliberating. Through Elihu, the man foreshadowing the coming age of the (Holy) Spirit, God reveals himself to be bigger than Job or his friends could ever conceive. Up to this point, Job and his friends had tried hard to explain God through limited human logic. Then, after encountering him personally, no questions remained.

Job's problems began when a great wind came upon his family; now, in another great wind, God made himself known to him. Through these two storms – one demonic and the other divine – Job was lifted above his self-righteousness and own wisdom and he began to see God as he truly is. God caught Job's attention through the first storm, and gave him time to discover that his own answers, and those of his friends, led nowhere at all. Then out of the second storm, God spoke and everything changed.

Not once during Job's troubles did God point out to him what had happened behind the scenes. Even when all was concluded God did not explain himself, Job simply encountered him and all was restored. Job asked no more questions. *My ears had heard of you*

OUT OF THE STORM
Becoming strong disciples

but now my eyes have seen you.[26] He had met God and that was enough.

Job's first storm was initiated by Satan. The first step to take in any storm, though, is always the same: to look to God, to fix our eyes on him and meet with him afresh. This comes as no surprise, since both Testaments are full of exhortations to do just that: to seek him, look at him, ask him, gaze at him, worship him, trust him, and set our hearts and minds on him. Interestingly, this is the opposite of what many do, which is to spend large parts of their lives focusing on themselves and looking inwards to solve stormy problems.

CHAPTER FIVE

Other storms

Nehemiah's determination to focus on God's calling and not be distracted, warded off the encroaching storm.

The Bible is full of literal and metaphorical storms. Elijah and Ezekiel encountered him in physical whirlwinds,[27] and his presence elsewhere is often described as God coming in a great wind – as in Isaiah 66.15; and Jeremiah 4.13. John the Baptist ended his life in a storm, as did Stephen and, according to tradition, many of the apostles. They all lost their lives following Christ. Hezekiah, Jeremiah, Isaiah and

---

[26] Job 42.5
[27] Though of course Elijah also met God in the stillness.

21

OUT OF THE STORM
Becoming strong disciples

many other prophets encountered storms along the way. And so did many kings of Israel.

Psalm 77 follows a similar pattern to the book of Job. The psalmist is in trouble. *Has God forgotten to be merciful? Has he in anger withheld his compassion?*[28] He then recalls how God had led Israel out of exile in Egypt. The storm language used here to describe the exodus perhaps helps us visualise the episode as Israel did: *I will meditate on all your works and consider all your mighty deeds ... The waters saw you, O God, the waters saw you and writhed; the very depths were convulsed. The clouds poured down water, the skies resounded with thunder, your arrows flashed back and forth. Your thunder was heard in the whirlwind, your lightning lit up the world; the earth trembled and quaked.*[29] God's redemption of Israel from Egypt took place in a storm. (How easy, I wonder, was it to follow Moses through the Red Sea against a backdrop of such thunder and lightning?) The psalm ends by acknowledging God in the storm: *Your path led through the sea...you led your people like a flock, by the hand of Moses and Aaron.*[30] As in Job, the agony of the storm, with all the accompanying questions to God, precedes the divine encounter. As the psalmist considers God, and the storm through

---

[28] **Psalm 77.9**
[29] **Psalm 77.12,16-18**
[30] **Psalm 77.19-20**

OUT OF THE STORM
Becoming strong disciples

which he led Israel, the need for any more answers simply goes away.

Nehemiah was threatened by a demonic storm, but saw it coming and was able to avoid it completely by keeping his eyes on the task at hand. *I'm engaged on a great project. why should I come down and talk to you?*[31] Should he have listened to Sanballat's invitations to meet him, or stopped his work to answer Sanballat's accusations, the resulting storm might well have engulfed him. Nehemiah's determination to focus on God's calling and not be distracted, warded off the encroaching storm. This is a great example of a storm that was avoided by being in the right place, doing the right thing, and using wise discernment.

By facing the real issue, i.e. that Sanballat was not sent by God but instead to distract and discourage him, Nehemiah successfully avoided God's work being delayed or even brought to a halt. He might have met with Sanballat, to discuss this or that... indeed why wouldn't a man of God go out of his way to respond to somebody's request to talk to him? But by discerning what lay behind the request, by using his spiritual insight (rather than merely fulfilling what many might have seen as his 'Christian' or pastoral responsibility), he made the tough but correct decision not to take his eyes off the work God had

---

[31] See *On The Chair*, a short course in this series, to receive encouragement on staying in the place God has put you.

given him. Not everyone who wants to speak to us is necessarily someone God wants us to spend time with. This too was a storm sent by God's enemies.

Chapter Six

God's ways

> *Whatever storm we go through, whether of our own making, Satan's or even through following God, ultimately it will be for God's glory, not our own.*

God's ways are not our ways! We don't understand where many of the storms we face come from, yet the prophet Nahum declared that *His way is in the whirlwind and the storm.*[32]

It is interesting that in each of the above scenarios, wherever the storm came from, the remedy is to look to God. An attack on our lives and ministries from Satan – for he does want to destroy us and our fruitfulness – is always best dealt with by looking up to God. Oh yes, we need to resist him actively, as James teaches us: *submit yourselves, then, to God. Resist the devil, and he will flee from you.*[33] Yet we can only do the if we do not take our eyes off God; Satan would be delighted if we were to focus on him.

Isaiah showed us a scene where the servant (who we now understand to be Christ), found himself in the dark. Isaiah exhorted him to cling to God, not to rely

---

[32] **Nahum 1.3c**
[33] **James 4.7**

OUT OF THE STORM
Becoming strong disciples

on anything that had helped him previously, even that which had formerly been a light for him.[34] Jesus would have been familiar with these verses and what they preach as he clung to his Father's words during his storm.

When we are in the middle of a storm, it can seem that we are in darkness, and that our usual strategies do not work. Neither the power of positive thinking, nor self-help books, nor particular spiritual routines, nor even our quiet times and prayer disciplines. It is as though God isn't there, as we thrash around for something or someone to help us during these times. Here, Isaiah exhorts us not to seek anything or anyone except God himself during these times, not resorting to any strategy or favourite method but to look to him alone, keeping our eyes and thoughts on him, trusting him. These are the times that he does his mightiest work in us. When we come through the darkness of the storm we will have been strengthened and next time we will lean less on our own understanding, and more easily on him.

A little earlier in Isaiah, we learn that God refines and tests us. Remarkably, on looking closer at the passage we discover it is not for our sakes that he does this. *See, I have refined you, though not as silver; I have tested you in the furnace of affliction. For my own sake, for my own sake I do this ... I will not yield my glory to*

---

[34] See Isaiah 50.10-11

OUT OF THE STORM
Becoming strong disciples

another.[35] Whatever storm we go through, whether of our own making, Satan's or even through following God, ultimately it will be for God's glory, not our own.

Maybe we cannot tell, when in the storm, where the storm came from, or maybe we can. If it's from Satan, we can ensure we are submitted to God, standing in the authority Christ has given us, and resisting him. If, on the other hand, we are running away from God's will for us – whether recently or long ago – and we now see that clearly, we need to repent, get right with God, and refuse to turn to the left or the right. The whale is on the way and God will turn it all for good. If it is a storm that has come simply through following him, or we don't know where it's come from, we can look to him, make sure we are right with him, stay focused on the work he has given us and cling to him and him alone. If we have been building our house wisely, and obediently living by Christ's word, our foundation of rock will ensure we will still be standing after the storm dies – keep going!

Will there be a people who overcome?

> He is seeking a people of faith who want to overcome by living 'in Christ' – no matter what storms come along.

This is a question that runs through the entire Bible: will God find a people who will live their lives for him, intentionally fixing their eyes up on him and living for his glory, just as Jesus once did? Will they learn to overcome the world, flesh and the devil – whatever storms come their way? Will they still move forwards

---

[35] Isaiah 48.10-11

OUT OF THE STORM
Becoming strong disciples

advancing the Kingdom no matter what they live through? In the new testament and the old, God sought such a people. He still does today: he is seeking a people of faith who want to overcome, by living 'in Christ' – no matter what storms come along – and regardless of where they have their origin. Even in the self-generated storms they will be able, like Jonah, to turn around, repent, and once more *look again toward your holy temple.*[36]

In the early chapters of Revelation we read of the risen, glorified Jesus addressing his church. In almost every letter to the seven churches he refers to the *overcomers* and what he or she will inherit:

> *To him who overcomes I will give the right to eat from the tree of life.*[37]
>
> *He who overcomes will not be hurt at all by the second death.*[38]
>
> *To him who overcomes I will give some of the hidden manna.*[39]
>
> *To him who overcomes and does my will to the end, I will give authority over the nations.*[40]

---

[36] **Jonah 2.4**
[37] **Revelation 2.7**
[38] **Revelation 2.11**
[39] **Revelation 2.17**
[40] **Revelation 2.26**

OUT OF THE STORM
Becoming strong disciples

> *He who overcomes will, like them [the saints who have not soiled their clothes], be dressed in white.*[41]

What are they to overcome? The world, flesh and the devil, and storms of every kind that these three dangers create for followers of God.

Their houses always stand firm.

APPENDIX

Corollary

- Those who were already God-centred, avoided or withstood the storm. (Paul, Jesus, Nehemiah) These were people who, like the wise builders, learned to hear what God was saying and obeyed.

- Even when we walk in obedience, there will still be storms. (Paul, Jesus, disciples)

- Walking in disobedience and running away from God, brings unnecessary storms. As soon as we truly repent, God begins redeeming the situations we've got ourselves into and sends immediate help to allow us to escape our storm. (Jonah)

- God is often encountered away from our everyday lives. Storms can lead to fresh brokenness and be places of divine encounter. In the middle of a

---

[41] Revelation 3.5

OUT OF THE STORM
Becoming strong disciples

storm we're often listening much more keenly and are more likely to obey what we hear.

- Following Jesus means walking into and through storms. (Disciples on lake Galilee)

What to do in a Storm

- If we're in a storm of our own making, having run from God in some way or other, repent. (This is not saying sorry, it's turning around and walking the other direction). Turn back to him and accept his deliverance however it comes. (Jonah)

- Do not give attention to anything or anyone trying to turn your attention away from where God has put you or from looking to him. (Nehemiah)

- Trust God and his promises, he's bigger than the storm. Look up to him! (Paul, Jesus)

- Stand firm. Remember the previous storms he's brought you through. Don't be afraid to follow him even if it's into a storm. (Israelites, Moses, disciples)

- Expect to encounter him in any storm. Look for him. Allow him to meet with you in whatever way he wants to. Allow yourself to be changed forever. (Job)

- Speak out to encourage others in the storm with his prophetic words of encouragement and prophetic words. Don't worry if they don't listen – they may later. (Paul)

OUT OF THE STORM
Becoming strong disciples

Standing in/Preventing the Storm

- Listen to his word and obey it – let this be your lifestyle – in the small things and bigger things, day by day. (Two builders)
- Regularly bring to mind the ways in which he has saved you in the past. Recall your victories and successes through following him.
- Cultivate an attitude of thankfulness. Stay humble. You always need to hear him; you will always need to obey him.

Pastors and Leaders

- Train and teach people to have faith – credal faith, salvation faith and living faith, based on God's word.
- Train them to hear God, and obey God,[42] and to learn to discern the storms heading their way.
- Teach them about spiritual authority so they learn to stand firm and speak boldly in the midst of the storm.
- Train them before and during storms, and whilst loving and empathising, don't resort to pastoring with merely human love and sympathy, but use their storms to train and strengthen them spiritually.

---

[42] **Matthew 28.20**

OUT OF THE STORM
Becoming strong disciples

Practical Help in a Storm

- Praise and worship – even when you don't feel like it. It's a sacrifice of praise and it's a choice. True praise and worship will always kick the devil in the teeth and help keep us Jesus focused.

- If the devil is the cause of any particular storm, resist him. Keep your eyes on God though.

- Throw off any and all concern about what others may be thinking – it doesn't matter. Keep your eyes on him and your spiritual armour on.

- Find one person of faith with whom you can be completely honest, including emotionally honest, without feeling you have to say the 'right thing'. Conversely, don't pour out to everyone how you're feeling. (This a good advice whether in a storm or not). Talk to this person regularly through the storm.

- Stay connected to God. Even if your regular times with him go awry, don't beat yourself up, but find time to pour out your heart to him, just like the psalmists who were brutally honest with him about what was going on. Remember Jesus died for the real you, not any mask you might be wearing.

- Like the psalmists, end on a note of faith! Remember the times of God's faithfulness and his victories in your life.

OUT OF THE STORM
Becoming strong disciples

- This is where your life up to this point is tested; stay Christ-centred. If you haven't felt close so far in your life, now is a good opportunity to put him in the right place.

- Keep eating, exercising and sleeping. If you wake in the night, get out of bed, go to another room and use the time to pray. There is something very different about praying in the stillness of the night. Be with him. Write down what he says to you. Have the Bible at your side. He will speak to you through it.

- Thank him, that he is the same God today as yesterday, that he is sovereign over all and that his promises are true, that he is as close during the storm as he is during the sunshine and blue sky. Read Psalm 91 –memorise parts of it.

- Live one day at a time. Today is the day of salvation. His mercies are new every morning.

- Know and believe that he's carrying you, even when it doesn't feel like it.

- Stay on your chair (seated in heavenly places, in Christ[43]). If you fall off, repent and get straight back on it again.

- When you're in the dark, remember what he said to you when you were in the light.

---

[43] See *On The Chair*, by Richard George, published by The Way of the Spirit 2012.

OUT OF THE STORM
Becoming strong disciples

- Be certain that he turns everything for the good of those who are called according to his purpose[44].
- Leave your worries, anxiety, concerns, fears and questions at the cross. Each time you pick them up, repent and leave them there again.

---

[44] Romans 8.28

2.

OUT OF THE STORM
PART TWO

Study Guide

These notes will help you to focus on the central themes of the Bible's story and stimulate further thought for discussion in groups and for personal application in life.

1. First, read the pages above corresponding to the section of notes you are about to use.

2. Second, read the passages at the head of the questions (if different). Now referring back to the booklet as required, answer all the questions.

3. Write down your answers, as briefly as possible, using only a few words, or at most a couple of sentences each time. As you do so, pray the Lord

OUT OF THE STORM
Becoming strong disciples

will show you how your reading and answers are to relate to your own life as a Christian.

4. If you discuss the readings in a group, try to stick to the set themes. It is so easy to go off at tangents, consider many interesting topics, and in the end miss the whole purpose of the study. The questions are to help you avoid doing that, by keeping your thoughts directed to the important, central issues.

5. If you use the recorded teaching that goes with this booklet, listen to it straight through in one sitting before you start your study; then perhaps listen again at the conclusion of your study.

6. In a group, do not hurry the study. Its purpose is to help you grow spiritually as well as in understanding, and that takes prayer as well as reading.

OUT OF THE STORM
Becoming strong disciples

WEEK ONE – INTRODUCTION AND JONAH (Pages 1 to 9)

1. **Matthew 8.18-27; 1Kings 19.19-21**
   Ignore the sub headings which were not part of the original manuscript. What is this passage in Matthew about?

   Leaving everything worldly that you rely on – The things of the world are dead – but I'm offering eternal life – → telling Matthew he was alive – chosen for eternal life.

   How would you feel if you were the man whose father had recently died and you heard Jesus say this to you? What do you think Jesus meant?

   This is your opportunity to answer his call – to follow the path to eternal life.

   How does it relate to the 1Kings passage, and what do the two together say about prophetic ministry?

   Leaving Livelyhood & everything that you trust & depend upon to follow Gods calling.

OUT OF THE STORM
Becoming strong disciples

2. **Matthew 7.24-9**

What is the precise difference between the wise and foolish builder?

Obedience

The rock is obedience to God will

What are you building your life upon? Explain.

Faith, hope, love

How would you help people in storms? If you were (are) a pastor, what does this passage say about your role?

OUT OF THE STORM
Becoming strong disciples

3. **Jonah 1.1-6**
Why did Jonah run away from God's command? What would you have done?

Have you ever run away? When?

Where did the storm come from? Compare Jonah's responses in the storm to Jesus' during the storm on the lake of Galilee.[45]

---

[45] Matthew 8:23-27

OUT OF THE STORM
Becoming strong disciples

4. **Jonah 1.7- 3.1; Acts 3.25**
   What was God waiting for from Jonah? Which verse brings about the change in Jonah's downward spiral?

   What was the difference in God's command to Jonah the second time (i.e. in 3.1)?

   How easy is it being a prophet? Who are today's prophets?

OUT OF THE STORM
Becoming strong disciples

You have an anointing from God. Why?

WEEK TWO – PAUL (Pages 10 to 13)

5. **Acts 24-27**
   Summarise the events leading up to Paul travelling to Rome. Tertullus give evidence to governor - Causing dissension among Jews - Jews wanted to try Paul. Couldn't decide what he had done wrong. He requested to go to Rome to be judged for his crime - He was taken on a ship that capsised on Malta

   What picture do you get of Paul's character from reading these events at sea? Paul had heavenly authority - Spoke with conviction

OUT OF THE STORM
Becoming strong disciples

What encouragements does Paul get as the storm develops? How was he able to stand so firm?

— a dream

Describe the storm in your own words. What resemblances are there to the storm Jonah found himself in?

The people tried to solve it for them selves.

How does the storm differ from Jonah's?

OUT OF THE STORM
Becoming strong disciples

6. **Acts 28**
   How did God use Paul on Malta? Why didn't he try to escape from his captors?

   How can the end of Acts be seen as a victory? What is Paul ministering, and how?

   Do you ever allow your circumstances to hinder doing what God has called you to? Be specific, about times in the past, and now/today, when you have or haven't allowed this to happen.

OUT OF THE STORM
Becoming strong disciples

WEEK THREE – JESUS (Pages 13 to 16)

uninfluencable unchangable

7. Luke 9.51; Mark 11
What was Jesus' state of mind, do you think, as he entered Jerusalem?

Complete trust in God – complete calm confidence

8. Luke 4; John 7; John 10.39;
How many times did men fail to kill/imprison Jesus when they attempted to? Why did they fail? Can you think of any further occasions when this happened?

1. cliff at Nazareth
2. John 7 - Feast in Judea - pharisees wanted him arrested
3. Seize + stone him
It was not yet his time – Other times Herod killing babies

9. Acts 21.1-26
Why did Paul not heed the warnings he was given?

He was "ready to die" at Jerusalem for the name of the Lord Jesus.

OUT OF THE STORM
Becoming strong disciples

10. **John 17.1**
    The hour for what has come? *It's finialy the time for Jesus to sacrafice his life on th cross according to God's will.*

WEEK FOUR – JOB (Pages 16 to 21)

11. **Job 1-2**
    What did Job lose as a result of Satan's two appearances before God in Heaven?

    What would you have replied to Job's wife if you had been him?

OUT OF THE STORM
Becoming strong disciples

12.   Job 32-33
How was Elihu different from Job's three friends?

Why do you think John McKay called Elihu a *proto-charismatic*?

13.   Job 7-8; 36-37
What or who is the focus of 7-8?

What or who is the focus of 36-37?

OUT OF THE STORM
Becoming strong disciples

14. Job 38-42

This is the first time since chapter one that God speaks. What does he say?

This is the second storm Job has experienced. How does it differ from the storm in 1-2?

What effect do God's words have on Job?

OUT OF THE STORM
Becoming strong disciples

Where does God explain to Job how the first storm came about? Why do you think Job stops asking God questions?

What can we learn from Elihu about how to help those going through storms?

WEEK FIVE – OTHER STORMS (Pages 21 to 24)

15. **Psalm 77**
    In what way is this Psalm reminiscent of what we read last week in Job?

[Handwritten notes:] 18 "Your voice of your thunder was in the whirlwind" Job 38 The Lord answered Job 'out of the whirlwind' remembering the mighty ness of God + God's dominion over everything.

OUT OF THE STORM
Becoming strong disciples

Which verse(s) do you identify with?

16. **Nehemiah 6-7**
What would you have said to Sanballat (6.2)?

What was Nehemiah's secret of success in seeing the project through?

What tactics were attempted against him, and how did he overcome them?

Passion Translation

OUT OF THE STORM
Becoming strong disciples

Have you ever been distracted from the work God has given you?

WEEK SIX – OVERCOMER (Pages 24 to 28)

17. **Isaiah 48.10-11; 50.10-11**
    Why do we suffer trials? For whom? *For God - He tests us in the furnace of affliction. God is looking for his people.*

    When we are in the darkness, what should we do? What shouldn't we do? Explain what this might mean for us when we're in a storm.
    Dnt rely on anything but the Lord - Never turn against the Lord to solve our problems. Learn to rely on God - not on our own understanding.

49

OUT OF THE STORM
Becoming strong disciples

18. **Revelation 2-3**
    How many times does Jesus refer to those who overcome? 7 times.

Those who overcome —
1 * I will give to eat from the tree of Life which is in the midst of the paradise of God.
2 It shall not be hurt by the second death
3 I will give some of the hidden manna to eat
4 Power over the nations.
5 Clothed in white garments + Name will remain in book of life

- the loveless ness
- The persecuted
- Compromise
- Corruption
- ~~Ash~~ Death

    What do they need to overcome? What do we?
    Be watchful
    Hold fast what you have
    repent.

19. **Read the Appendix (Pages 28 to 33)**
    What are the three main things you have learned over these weeks about going through storms?

Revelation
  5 - v. 8
  8 - v 3-4

OUT OF THE STORM
Becoming strong disciples

What have you learned about preventing them?

You can't prevent all storms they will always happen but you can avoid unnecessary storms by following God.

What are you going to do about what you have learned?

Use the time I wake up in the night for prayer - start keeping a prayer journal.

THE WAY OF THE SPIRIT

The Way of the Spirit has a series of Bible reading and study programmes, giving a guide to the whole Bible as seen through the activity and experience of the Holy Spirit.

HOME AND FURTHER STUDY COURSES

Various levels of study and training are available, including short Bible Reading courses similar to this one, and the full-length Reading Course that covers the whole Bible in four six-month parts.

Discipleship training and training for Bible teachers includes full-time residential courses, part-time courses with short residential schools, and mentored training that you can take in local groups and seminars.

For more information **email resources@thewayofthespirit.com**, or go to **www.thewayofthespirit.com/training_overview/**